D1212336

One Cool Watermelon

Please visit our Web site at: www.garethstevens.com
For a free color catalog describing Gareth Stevens Publishing's
list of high-quality books and multimedia programs, call
1-800-542-2595 (USA) or 1-800-387-3178 (Canada).
Gareth Stevens Publishing's fax: (414) 332-3567.

Library of Congress Cataloging-in-Publication Data

Tofts, Hannah.
    One cool watermelon / Hannah Tofts; photography by Rupert Horrox. — U.S. ed.
        p. cm.
    ISBN-13: 978-0-8368-7488-4 (lib. bdg.)
    ISBN-13: 978-0-8368-8143-1 (softcover)
    1. Counting—Juvenile literature. I. Horrox, Rupert, ill. II. Title.
QA113.T655   2007
513.2'11—dc22   2006029882

This edition first published in 2007 by
Gareth Stevens Publishing
A Member of the WRC Media Family of Companies
330 West Olive Street, Suite 100
Milwaukee, Wisconsin 53212 USA

This edition copyright © 2007 by Gareth Stevens, Inc.
Text copyright © 2006 by Zero to Ten Limited. Illustrations © 1998 by
Hannah Tofts. First published by Zero to Ten, an imprint of Evans Brothers
Limited, 2A Portman Mansions, Chiltern Street, London W1U 6NR, United
Kingdom. This U.S. edition published under license from Evans Brothers Limited.

Gareth Stevens editor: Dorothy L. Gibbs
Gareth Stevens art direction and design: Tammy West

Printed in the United States of America

1 2 3 4 5 6 7 8 9 10 10 09 08 07 06

One Cool Watermelon

Hannah Tofts

Photography by Rupert Horrox

GARETH**STEVENS**

GS PUBLISHING

A Member of the WRC Media Family of Companies

In my kitchen I have . . .

one cool watermelon

2 two round potatoes

3

three fuzzy kiwifruits

4 **four** yellow bananas

5

five shiny apples

6 six **six** bushy broccoli tops

7

seven juicy oranges

8 eight sweet
bell peppers

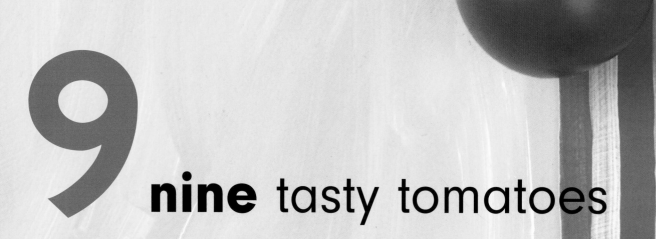

9
nine tasty tomatoes

10 ten plump peaches

and I like to
eat them all!